PRAISE FOR LIBERTY AT RISK

"I love it — *Liberty at Risk* illustrates so many important principles of libertarianism with reference to current affairs and basic good common sense too. It is exactly the sort of book that will reach out to people who unbeknown to themselves are instinctively libertarians — people who understand that the good life comes from the lived experience not subservience to government.

I was particularly taken by the line, "If we wish to convince others that our ideology is superior, then firstly we must understand its concepts and its roots, and secondly we must live its truth". Magnificent. This book will go a long way to helping us understand liberal roots and concepts."

- Sinclair Davidson, Professor, Institutional Economics, RMIT University

"Never has a book been more timely and welcomed than *Liberty at Risk: Tackling Today's Political Problems*. Australian Peter Fenwick addresses some of the most important and vexing problems of today in 23 short chapters. The answers rest on the foundations of Classical Liberalism and Austrian free market economics and the reader will be reminded of work of the great Henry Hazlitt. An excellent introduction for the uninitiated."

- Dr. Mark Thornton, Senior Fellow, Ludwig von Mises Institute

"Peter Fenwick challenges our perception of society's status quo. He does not espouse a new age philosophy, but uses the philosophies of the 18th and 19th century libertarians whose thinking influenced our democracies in their infancy.

He questions the distortions of their ideals that are now causing rifts and failures in our modern day world.

While our current politicians, bureaucrats and business leaders maybe beyond change, these essays provide food for thought to stimulate the next generation to change our world for a better future.

Topics such as the role and responsibilities of government, the distortion of crony capitalism, the rights of lobby groups to peddle self-interest, tolerance, entrepreneurs, caliphates, the role of the family, accepting responsibility...the list goes on. But in itself it provides a curriculum for any University, year 11 or year 12 current affairs or philosophy program that all of us would love to join."

 - Dr Hugh Seward, Chairman of the Council of The Geelong College Adjunct Senior Research Fellow at Monash University

"Fenwick explores how the principles of libertarianism have been undermined by the rise of the welfare state and the increasingly interventionist governments of Western democracies. He writes of crony capitalism; the decline in civil virtues; how governments repeatedly attempt to solve social issues by regulation; and the rise of jihadist Islamism.

If you like food for thought, then this book is a feast! But it's not burgers and fries; rather it's a collection of small, appetizing and healthy entrees that will whet your appetite for the main course — Peter Fenwick's book *The Fragility of Freedom — Why Subsidiarity Matters.*"

 - Graham Haines, Principal Consultant, Plans to Reality

"Peter Fenwick writes what so many of us think—he poses commonsense responses to even the most complex economic and political issues. In essence, a free market, and the freedom of individuals to act responsibly on their own behalf, should result in a better outcome for all.

Sadly, ego, pride and greed come into play, and these forces cannot operate as they should. If only politicians and big business could/would read Peter's work, examine history and learn from it, then inevitably our world would be a better place.

We probably recognize that the moral goals of the welfare state are not all wrong. It is the questions of what constitute our inalienable rights, and the methods used to ensure those rights, which distinguish libertarianism from socialist democracy.

What needs to be determined is to what extent the goals of the welfare state in terms of ensuring shelter, basic income, education, health (etc.) should constitute essential rights of the individual. And further, having been so determined — they should be guaranteed as a universal right to all, not selectively and inefficiently delivered by a bloated bureaucracy.

At least, if each of us reads Peter's work, and seriously take responsibility for ourselves and our families, and deliberates the notion of balance and fairness, then the notion of changing the world one person (our self) at a time, may make it that better place for all of us."

- Susan M. Renouf, Executive Director, Renouf & Associates

"Peter Fenwick's new book should be read by everyone who is concerned with the current world's problems. His insight in selecting the problems and presenting alternatives in a simple manner is extraordinary. The new format makes easy reading about difficult problems."

- John Link, CEO, Link Pumps and Engineering

Liberty at Risk
Tackling Today's
Political Problems

PETER FRANCIS FENWICK

LIBERTY
AT *Risk*

TACKLING
TODAY'S
POLITICAL
PROBLEMS

Connor Court Publishing

Published in 2016 by Connor Court Publishing Pty Ltd

Connor Court Publishing Pty Ltd
PO Box 7257
Redland Bay QLD 4165
sales@connorcourt.com
www.connorcourt.com
Phone 0497 900 685

ISBN: 9781925501162

Front Cover Design: Manish414

Front Cover Photo: Francisco Diez

Printed in Australia

This book is dedicated to Ludwig von Mises and Robert Nozick who sparked my interest in Austrian Economics and Libertarian Philosophy fifty years ago. Their major works, Mises' *Human Action* and Nozick's *Anarchy, State, and Utopia* are still in print and are having a major influence on today's young scholars.

CONTENTS

INTRODUCTION

Libertarianism[1] is the political philosophy of individual liberty. It is based on the principle of private property and founded on natural rights theory as expounded by John Locke in the seventeenth century. One hundred years later, Locke's work had a profound influence on the American Declaration of Independence.

> We hold these truths to be self-evident, that all men are created equal, that they are endowed by their Creator with certain unalienable Rights, that among these are Life, Liberty and the Pursuit of Happiness.

Over the years, many great thinkers have contributed to this political philosophy, including David Hume, Adam Smith, Mary Wollstonecraft[2], John Stuart and Harriet Taylor Mill, Frederic Bastiat, F.A. Hayek, Milton Friedman, Ayn Rand, Ludwig von Mises, Murray Rothbard, and Robert Nozick.

Libertarian theory argues that individual rights flow from our inherent human dignity, our self-ownership. We own ourselves and this gives us certain rights, in particular rights to life, liberty and the fruits of our labour. These rights constrain others, and so protect us from being killed or maimed, forced to work against our will, or infantilized. Furthermore, we are entitled to exchange the things we own with anyone who perceives value in them.

So that sums up the libertarian creed: self-ownership, private property and the free market. In practice, this leads to a society of co-operation, tolerance and mutual respect, a preference for voluntary organisations, and a minimal role for the state.

In a libertarian society, it becomes honourable to be in commerce, to work hard and to innovate. Society comes to admire the entrepreneur who identifies consumer needs and finds economic ways to fulfil them. There is liberty and dignity for ordinary people. Consequently, large numbers of people are empowered and the bourgeois virtues — faith, hope, love, courage, temperance, justice and prudence — are valued, encouraged and honoured.

Wherever this ideology has been tried, mankind has flourished. Per capita incomes have risen multiple times, longevity has increased by many years, education has become universally available, women have been treated equally, there has been more time devoted to culture and the arts, and there has been noticeable increases in civility. Elsewhere, throughout history, only small ruling elites led the good life; the majority led a precarious and unpleasant existence.

Unfortunately, over the past hundred years the social democratic welfare state has inhibited progress in the West, and now theocratic Islamists are creating mayhem in the Middle East.

The twenty-three commentaries that follow discuss the errors of these flawed ideologies from a libertarian perspective.

1

THE EMPEROR'S CLOTHES

Throughout the Western world, the welfare state has been exposed as economically unsustainable. The regulatory and coercive powers of the state have been captured by sectional interests for their own economic benefit.

The state has become pervasive in our lives. We have lost the belief that we can do things ourselves. We live with the peculiar notion that if we cannot afford some desired service, it should be provided by the government. So government spending expands as everyone seeks funding for their every wish.

The consequences are unmanageable debt, unsound money, poor investment decisions, and unfair burdens on the productive, the thrifty and the young.

No amount of tinkering at the edges will solve this problem. The flaws are fundamental and systemic.

It is time we admitted that the emperor has no clothes.[3]

2

THE IMPOSSIBLE PROMISES OF
OUR POLITICIANS

Fifty per cent of Australian households now receive more in welfare benefits than they pay in income tax. The proportion rises to eighty if you include government contributions for health and education. Now that the majority of voters are the beneficiaries of state largesse, has it become politically impossible to unwind middle-class welfare?

The 2015 Intergenerational Report, produced by the Australian Treasury, highlighted problems that astute writers such as Tom Woods[4] have known for a long time. The social democratic welfare state is financially unsustainable:

> All over the world, the impossible promises governments have made to their populations are beginning to unravel. Millions of people have arranged their lives in the expectation of various forms of government support that will be mathematically impossible to provide.

The Intergenerational Report states that:

> The Australian Government is currently spending over $100 million a day more than it collects, and is borrowing to meet the shortfall. ... The policies currently legislated would not see the

budget in surplus at any point over the next 40 years.

Fixing this is not easy. All attempts to reduce government spending are met with vigorous political campaigns from those personally affected. Has it become a politically impossible task?

3

UNDERMINING A FREE SOCIETY

Most people have great difficulty coming to grips with the moral failures of the welfare state and its financial unsustainability. Reform is going to require courage, intellectual honesty and a willingness to admit that deeply held beliefs are wrong.

> We are ready to accept almost any explanation of the present crisis in our civilization except one: that the present state of the world may be the result of genuine error on our part and that the pursuit of some of our most cherished ideals has apparently produced results utterly different from those we expected.[5]

Yuval Levin, Hertog Fellow at the Ethics and Public Policy Centre in Washington, clearly articulates what is wrong. It is a good starting point for serious discussion of issues that cannot be ignored and must be addressed:

> Moreover, because all citizens — not only the poor — become recipients of benefits, people in the middle class come to approach their government as claimants, not as self-governing citizens, and to approach the social safety net not as a great majority of givers eager to make sure that a small minority of recipients are

spared from devastating poverty, but as a mass of dependents demanding what they are owed. It is hard to imagine an ethic better suited to undermining the moral basis of a free society.[6]

4

THE SWEDISH MODEL FAILED TOO

Bernie Sanders candidacy for Presidency of the USA has put socialism back on the political agenda. How could such a failed ideology garner so much support — particularly from the young?

Ludwig von Mises said socialism wouldn't work. And it didn't. He pointed out that without the price mechanism it is impossible to allocate resources efficiently and to make choices between economic alternatives. He explained that seventy years before the Berlin Wall fell.

The students who today support Sanders were not alive to witness the failure of communism in post-war USSR and Eastern Europe.

> On 9 November 1989, the Berlin Wall fell and the communist experiment was over. Established with so much hope and intellectual support, it had delivered poverty, destroyed trust among its citizens, and terrorized, censored and imprisoned those who disagreed with the party line.[7]

Supporters of socialism will tell you that it differs from the communism that failed so spectacularly. They will not even consider the Nazi version — National Socialism — which had such an evil impact on Western Europe. And North Korea and Venezuela are not held up as exemplars. Today's supporters prefer the Swedish model.

The Swedes, the Danes and the Norwegians enjoy a high standard of living and a stress-free lifestyle in an egalitarian society. Yes, they pay high taxes, but this welfare state is Utopia. This is the model that Paul Krugman[8] and Bernie Sanders are hoping will become the standard for America.

The problem is, it is not true. The Swedish model has failed. Let me tell you about it. But firstly, let us review a little history.

In 1850, Sweden was one of the poorest countries in the world. Over the next hundred years, income increased eight times and the population doubled. Infant mortality fell from 15 to 2 per cent and life expectancy increased by 28 years. By 1950, Sweden was the fourth richest country in the world.

The benefits that began in 1850 had their genesis in the work of Anders Chydenius whose advocacy of a free market and a minimal state preceded Adam Smith by eleven years. His support for freedom of the press in 1766 had a crucial influence on Sweden's economic development. In the early nineteenth century, it enabled Lars Johan Hierta to establish an evening newspaper, *Aftonbladet*, in which he promoted his views of classical liberalism — especially the right to private property and equal treatment before the law. This led to significant practical changes.

Between 1849 and 1865, joint-stock company law was introduced, banks were allowed to be established and interest rates were deregulated. Regulations restricting the iron and timber industries were lifted, the guild system was abolished, and it became easier to start a business. Immigration and emigration were permitted, education became more universally available, and women were permitted to own and inherit property, be educated and to have a career.

These changes created a fruitful environment for entrepreneurs. Most of Sweden's great companies were established around the turn of the century, including Atlas Copco (1873), L.M. Ericsson (1876), ASEA (1883), Alfa Laval (1883), Scania (1891), AGA (1904), SKF (1907), and Electrolux (1910).

So Sweden thrived. It also benefitted by staying out of two world wars.

The Social Democratic Party came to power in 1932 and dominated Swedish politics for most of the rest of the century. They began cautiously, maintaining capitalist institutions, and working to keep big business and the middle class on side. By 1950, taxes were still lower and the public sector smaller than comparable countries.

It was later, in the fifties, sixties and seventies, that welfare state policies were implemented. Between 1950 and 1980, public spending rose from 19 to 60 per cent of GDP. And that is when it all started to unravel. The scope of government benefits expanded, rigid labour market regulations were introduced, stagnating sectors of the economy were propped up and taxes dramatically increased. Growth rates declined. The currency had to be devalued. By 1990, the public sector had increased by over a million employees, but not one net private sector job had been created in forty years. Compared to the USA, by the end of the 1990s, the median household income was two-thirds and the proportion of the adult population with a bachelor degree was about half.

There have been other adverse social effects. There has been a decline in the institution of marriage; a high proportion of adults now live alone. Children are brought up by the state not their parents. Crime rates have increased, particularly violent crime. Swedish academic, Per Bylund, bemoans the loss of bourgeois virtues. Within two generations, he writes, Swedes went from being a proud, hard-working and self-reliant people to a nation of immature, irresponsible, needy, spoiled and utterly demanding individuals.[9]

Sweden's wealth in the middle of the twentieth century was due to the intellectual input of men such as Chydenius and Hierta, and the operation of a free market economy from 1850 to 1950. While the Social Democrats kept a free market economy in place the country remained wealthy. But when they thought that they could squander its capital on cradle to grave welfare they quickly destroyed everything. It took less than 30 years to drop from the fourth richest country in the world to the fourteenth.

In recent years, Sweden has reduced taxes, privatized sectors of the economy and reformed its pension system. It is publicly honouring Chydenius and Hierta. Things are looking up. They have recognised that the Swedish model failed.

5

CRONY CAPITALISM

Many works by the great Australian sculptor Geoffrey Bartlett[10] juxtapose contrasting elements in surprising ways, delighting the senses and challenging the intellect.

Likewise, I wish to surprise you with the proposition that the apparent evils of capitalism are the consequences of the principles of the social democratic welfare state.

Many modern business corporations do not, in fact, operate in the free market. They use government intervention to provide subsidies, inhibit agile competitors, fund their research and development, give them monopoly positions, enable them to profit from extremely risky positions, and to bail them out when they become 'too big to fail'. They use lobbyists to curry favours and to buy influence. By their actions, they give capitalism a bad name.

But what they do is not capitalism. It is not the workings of the free market. It is coercion. It is the taking of resources from citizens who have earned them legitimately, and redirecting them to benefit powerful friends. Some have termed it crony capitalism. That at least makes an important distinction.

The most egregious examples in recent history were the bailing out of the Wall Street banks and the automotive companies by the US government in 2008. Hank Paulsen, Secretary of Treasury and formerly with Goldman Sachs, falsely convinced Congress that the failure of the Wall Street banks would lead to the failure of the whole American economy. The CEOs of the automotive companies famously came to Washington in their private jets to plead for government help.

Why does this happen? Why do politicians provide funds, tax relief, favourable contracts, and exemption from regulations etc. to large companies? In general, it is to help with their own re-election. Most commonly this takes the form of the funding of political parties or the promise to create jobs. Sometimes the bribes are personal.

In modern democracies wealth is often used to influence political decisions. Developers bribe local councillors, or planning staff, to get favourable zoning provisions. In the USA, congressmen are beholden to wealthy backers who fund their expensive election campaigns. Governments bail out large companies in trouble, ostensibly to protect jobs.

But there is no economic logic in this. If large, well-managed, well-capitalised companies such as Ford, Shell and Alcoa — I single these out because, in recent years, they shed jobs in my home town of Geelong — determine that their businesses are not viable, then how does it become a good investment for our taxes? The effect is the same if it is Wall Street banks, automobile companies or a chocolate factory. Scarce resources are diverted to win votes or to benefit wealthy friends of government.

In practice, the welfare state has not worked out as intended. Most of the benefits have been captured by sections of the middle class. The principle of allowing government to enrich some persons at the expense of others is the root of the problem. The belief that one is entitled to the property of others has led to a decline in virtuous behaviours such as responsibility, love, hope, charity, prudence, justice, fortitude, thrift, diligence, industriousness, reliability, trustworthiness, courage, civility, generosity, hospitality, duty and honour.

Crony capitalism is spawned by the welfare state. It is the capture of state largesse by those with power. It can only be addressed by being prepared to admit that the political doctrines that have given us the welfare state have failed us politically, economically and morally.

We should heed the advice of Robert Nozick, in his famous treatise *Anarchy, State, and Utopia*:

> *The illegitimate use of a state by economic interests for their own ends is based upon pre-existing illegitimate power of the state to enrich some persons at the expense of others.*[11]

6

MINIMUM WAGES DENY JOBS TO OUR YOUTH

In March 2015, when Australia's Productivity Commission suggested that minimum wages and penalty rates might be subject to review, the ACTU[12] hit the airwaves and the streets to defend their hard won rights. They claimed that the proposals were offensive — rights that had been won by physical, economic and political coercion were not to be trammelled by rational debate.

Those most adversely affected by minimum wages are those out of work, those for whom the jobs do not exist at that rate. They are not members of trade unions; the unions have no concern for them.

Wage controls are a specific case of price controls and a most insidious one. If an employer is obliged to pay higher than the market rate, then the chances are the job will not exist. If it does, it will be in a marginal business at risk of going broke. Then the job will disappear.

Fixing minimum wage rates leads to unemployment. The government that regulates wages must inevitably bear the burden of unemployment benefits created by its own policy. Minimum wage rates, whether enforced by government decree or by labour union pressure and compulsion, are useless if they fix wage rates at the market level. But if they try to raise wage rates above the level an unhampered labour market would have determined, they result in permanent unemployment of a greater part of the potential labour force.

The concept of the minimum wage grew out of the concern that wages needed to be sufficient for a man to provide food, shelter, education and medical services for his family. A wage needed to be sufficient for the dignity of man. In Australia, in 1907, the Conciliation and Arbitration Court brought down the famous Harvester Judgment, which established the basic wage. This became the foundation for controlled wages for decades. Justice Higgins concluded that a basic wage of 42 shillings ($4.20) per week, or seven shillings per day, for an unskilled man was the minimum amount that he and his family could live on. This was an increase of 6 shillings a week or 17 per cent. Unfortunately, this well-meaning decision misunderstands the interplay of prices in an economy and the consequences for job creation. It is all very well to have a higher wage, but that applies only if you have a job. Also, as wages are the major component of goods and services, higher wages lead to higher prices; a foolish and unending spiral.

Minimum wages and restrictions on an employer's ability to fire poor performers favour those in work at the expense of those out of work. This dissuades entrepreneurs from creating jobs. It creates unemployment. It particularly disadvantages the young who miss out on the work experience and training that would qualify them for better jobs. In most Western countries, unemployment among the young is often two to four times the average level.

There is substantial evidence that many low-wage workers are in relatively high-income households and that poor households are usually poor because members of the households are out of work. Under this view, facilitating jobs growth should take precedence over raising wages of those in work. Minimum wage laws should not be seen as benign. They are a curse. They rob the young of self-esteem, of purpose and of life. They maintain households in poverty.

If we wish to increase wages, then we need a better mechanism. Henry Hazlitt[13] explains:

> We cannot distribute more wealth than is created. We cannot in the long run pay labour as a whole more than it produces. The best way to raise wages, therefore, is to raise marginal labour productivity. This can be done by many methods: by an increase in capital accumulation — i.e. by an increase in the machines with which the workers are aided; by new inventions and improvements; by more efficient management on the part of the employers; by more industriousness and efficiency on the part of workers; by better education and training.
>
> The more the individual worker produces, the more he increases the wealth of the whole community. The more he produces, the more his services are worth to consumers, and hence to employers. And the more he is worth to his employers, the more he will be paid. Real wages come out of production, not out of government decrees.

Minimum wages are keeping our youth out of work and out of the experiences that would lead to better future employment. We should resist the efforts of vested interests to retain their preferred position. Let the rational debate proceed. Let us give our young people a fair go.

7

BEING RESPONSIBLE FOR OURSELVES AND OUR FAMILIES

I wonder why the focus of our solutions for social problems seems to be to ask strangers to deal with them and government to fund them.

The incidence of family violence in Broken Hill is met by calls to restore funding of a legal aid facility. The incidence of vandalism by 12-year olds in Kununurra is met by calls for improved juvenile detention facilities.

In both cases, attention to the root causes of the problems might be more effective – minimizing or preventing the problems rather than treating the consequences. In both cases, one wonders what family, friends, neighbours and workmates were doing to allow such anti-social behaviour to persist.

Is there no one prepared to take responsibility?

Is there no one prepared to tell the wife-basher, 'Mate, this is not acceptable behaviour'?

Is there no family, friend or neighbour prepared to offer the bashed wife a helping hand?

Is there no one prepared to take 12-year old boys aside, inculcate social values and give them more productive activities, tasks and responsibilities so that they can mature into good citizens?

What are the parents doing? What are the grandparents doing? What are the friends and neighbours doing? Is there no one who cares for these young people and their future life?

Has the welfare state sapped our moral strength? Do we believe that all problems can be addressed by strangers and paid for by others?

8

CHARITY

We shall not be free if we are not compassionate. We should always be ready to assist those experiencing hardships, particularly unanticipated ones such as the loss of a job or a death in the family. We should want to provide ways to help those suffering from trauma, or mental or chronic health problems.

Whether delivered by government departments or contracted out, our current welfare systems do not work well. Many former charities have morphed into large not-for-profit organisations, which provide service delivery on behalf of government. In the process, they have lost their identity. Like all mature bureaucracies, they have turned their focus internally onto their own needs. They have lost the personal touch, that capacity for service that is the hallmark of the voluntary organisation. Dependent on government funding, they have become lobbyists for statist policies.

The state is not the appropriate institution for delivering compassion. It provides inefficient, untargeted and impersonal delivery of services. It diminishes virtuous behaviour. Gratitude is replaced by a sense of entitlement and mutual respect vanishes.

Charity is better delivered by small, local, caring, voluntary organisations than by large, remote, condescending, bureaucratic, government agencies.

9

LEADERS WE CAN TRUST

When Vaclav Havel died in 2011, tens of thousands of Czech citizens paid their respects. It is rare for a politician to be so loved. Havel was a man of great integrity who spent his life 'living the truth' in a society that was 'living a lie'.

Born in Prague in 1936, Vaclav Havel became an internationally recognised poet and playwright. He spent much of his life railing against the communist government and spent over five years in jail for his dissidence. When the regime fell in 1989, he became President of Czechoslovakia and was subsequently President of the Czech Republic for 10 years after the split with Slovakia.

In *Summer Meditations*, written eighteen months into his first presidency, he reflects on the evil behaviours that years of totalitarian rule had instilled in his citizens, and contemplates how to address them. He concludes that a moral and intellectual state cannot be established through a constitution, law or directives, but only through a constant stress on moral deliberation and moral judgement. This is a fine treatise by a fine man. It is full of wisdom from a life well-lived. It is well worth reading.

Some time ago, I wrote the following text, which became part of the back cover for my book *The Fragility of Freedom: Why Subsidiarity Matters:*

> ... the coercive and regularity powers of the state have been captured by sectional interests for their own benefit, leading to corruption in public life and crony capitalism in business. Civil virtues have declined throughout the community with leaders in politics, religion, business and the trade unions often abusing positions of trust.

Every day I am confronted, in our newspapers and on our TV news and current affairs programs, with more examples of leaders abusing positions of trust. Is it getting worse? Or have I simply become more aware of it?

Where are the leaders of the moral stature of Vaclav Havel today? Who would you nominate as a leader that your children could look up to?

10

EMPOWERED COMMUNITIES

Noel Pearson is admired as one of Australia's great political leaders and thinkers. In March 2015, he released a 165-page document *Empowered Communities: Empowered Peoples* recommending radical changes to government policies for Indigenous Australians.

Instead of policies being determined by bureaucrats in our capital cities and delivered by a largely non-Indigenous support industry, the report calls for the decision-making and its execution to be devolved to empowered communities.

The idea is that the principle of subsidiarity should apply. As Craig Ingrey of the La Perouse Local Aboriginal Land Council explained:

> The goal is to help individuals be more responsible for their families and themselves.

Pearson's report is timely. Social policies for Indigenous Australians have not delivered positive outcomes. Despite millions of dollars being spent over the past fifty years, serious disadvantage persists. Attempts to 'close the gap' have failed. In many communities, children are not getting an education, health is poor and life expectancy is low. There is a lot of drug abuse and violence, employment opportunities are few or non-existent and there is an entrenched culture of welfare dependence.

Although Indigenous Australians represent only 3 per cent of the population, they represent over 27 per cent of the prison population and this is rising – up from 20 per cent a decade ago.

The current expenditure of over $43,000 per head is not delivering value for the government or for the recipients. If we are honest, we have to admit that the system is not working and may be fundamentally flawed.

Over the years, a support industry has emerged. Pearson is critical of this:

> Our service delivery system promotes and exacerbates passivity. It doesn't actually do any good for the people the services are directed towards.

According to him, about 70 cents in the dollar goes to administration of programs by non-Indigenous staff. One can expect much criticism of Pearson from this quarter as their livelihood is threatened by his proposals.

The Empowered Communities concept is about Indigenous people taking greater responsibility and developing their own plans for change. It is led by Indigenous people, for Indigenous people in eight regions across Australia: North East Arnhem Land in the Northern Territory; Sydney and the Central Coast of NSW; the Murray Goulburn region in Victoria; the Cape York Peninsula in Queensland; the East and West Kimberley regions of Western Australia; and the NPY lands in the Central Desert region.

The Empowered Communities report proposes that Indigenous-led responsibility is crucial to effective and sustainable reform, and that cultural norms should be re-established to combat social dysfunction. These include that:

Children attend school every day, are on time, and are school ready

Children and those who are vulnerable are cared for and safe

Capable adults participate in training or work

People abide by conditions related to their tenancy in public housing – they maintain their homes, and pay their rent

People do not commit domestic violence, alcohol and drug offences, or petty crimes.

All of this is consistent with my own conclusions that services are better provided by small, local, caring, voluntary organisations than by large, remote, condescending, bureaucracies, and that society is improved if individuals take responsibility for themselves and their families and behave as good citizens within their communities.

11

SUBSIDIARITY

If we wish to create a society which will help citizens to achieve their human potential and happiness, we need to ensure that individuals are responsible for their own actions, that they respect the rights of others and that they know they are not entitled to anything they have not earned.

We need to put the family in its rightful place as the central economic unit in our society. We need to nurture the formation of families and help them to survive difficult times. We need to inculcate the concept that family members have responsibilities to love and support each other, and that those family relationships endure.

We need to restructure our society to limit the role of government to those essential activities that cannot be done otherwise. A good society should encourage the formation of voluntary associations and should not impede them unless they pose a threat to society. To achieve these things, some changes will be structural; others will involve changing cultural norms.

Subsidiarity is the principle of devolving decisions to the lowest practical level, that what individuals are able to do, society should not take over, and what smaller societies can do, larger societies should not take over.

Its advocates range from Alexis de Tocqueville in 1835 to Pope John Paul II in 1991[14]. It facilitates a wider range of solutions, quicker and more informed decision-making, and greater involvement of more citizens. There is less chance of one bad decision causing a systemic failure and less opportunity for moral hazard.

We do whatever we can ourselves, with our family, friends and neighbours. We form voluntary organizations – businesses, clubs and societies – so that like-minded citizens can achieve their common objectives. We keep government activity as local as possible, jointly funding only those activities that the group agree to be valuable, keeping citizens closely involved in what is relevant to them. The benefits of subsidiarity are numerous:

> Liberty is enhanced. If you can do something yourself, or with a few colleagues, in the way you want without harming your fellow citizens, then you do not have to submit to a less preferable, majority view.
>
> The ability of more citizens is used by society to devise solutions.
>
> There is more variety of solutions, with not just one majority view but lots of minority views.
>
> Others can see what works well, and what does not, and change their course to suit.
>
> Solutions can be implemented more quickly because you do not have to spend time convincing those in authority before you can act.
>
> If you get it wrong, you can fix it easily because its scope is more limited.
>
> More citizens are involved in the life of the society. They gain experiences in leadership, decision-making and working together.

12

IN PRAISE OF FAMILY BUSINESS

In his 1954 classic, *The Practice of Management*, Peter Drucker[15] wrote that 'the purpose of a business is to create customers'. It is a wonderful insight. In contrast, the nightly fare on *A Current Affair* or *Today Tonight* always includes stories about businessmen who are ripping off their unsuspecting customers – overcharging, or providing dodgy products, or charging for services not supplied.

Recently, when staying at our son's house in Sydney, I tried using Julian's exercise bike. Unfortunately, the pedals were slipping, so I visited Exagym, where Julian had purchased the bike, expecting to buy a replacement part for one that had worn out. The proprietor, Chris Quinn, quickly diagnosed the problem, checked the details of Julian's bike and his address, and volunteered to come around and fix the problem. This he did, and then he declined my offer of payment saying, 'it is all part of the service'.

As we chatted, I found out that Exagym was part of Infiniti Fitness Systems, a family business founded by his father in 1982. I was not surprised. Many of our clients at my consulting business, Fenwick Software, are family businesses, some into the second or third generation. Colleagues such as David Bilston at MFB who make steel cabinets, Adam Hazeldene at Hazeldene's Chicken

Farms and Helen Ward at Ward McKenzie, who make the bi-carb soda we all have in our pantries, instinctively understand Peter Drucker's wisdom. They have been looking after their clients well for decades.

Vaclav Havel wrote:

> It is a great mistake to think that the marketplace and morality are mutually exclusive. Precisely the opposite is true: the marketplace can work only if it has its own morality – a morality generally enshrined in laws, regulations, traditions, experiences, and customs.[16]

Any business that behaves unethically, or illegally, or simply not in the interest of its customers fails because very soon it has no customers.

So next time you see one of the rip-off stories on TV, check the longevity of the business. In many cases, you will find that the business is bankrupt, or in receivership, or simply not operating anymore. And the proprietors will be gone or in hiding, and certainly unwilling to talk to journalists.

Family businesses operate on a value system of doing the right thing by the customer. It is in their blood. That is why they thrive and grow.

13

HONOURING ENTREPRENEURS

Entrepreneurs create jobs. So if we want more jobs then we have to create an environment in which entrepreneurs flourish. The converse is also true; if there are insufficient jobs being created it is because the conditions for entrepreneurs are not sufficiently conducive.

The conventional wisdom is somewhat different. Our politicians promote themselves as the ones who create jobs, and presumably most people believe this. It is worth considering in what ways politicians create jobs.

Firstly, they can increase the number of public sector jobs. Depending on your worldview you may see this in a positive or negative light. You may applaud a government that increases the numbers of nurses and teachers for instance, but baulk at increases in those performing administrative functions. The reality is that large bureaucracies are inefficient and unresponsive. This is especially so in education and health which are two areas of our economy that have not experienced cost reductions from innovation in the past fifty years. Increasing the size of the public sector tends to reduce prosperity.

Secondly, they can support businesses that promise to create or maintain jobs. They are particularly prone to do this in marginal electorates. But if these businesses need government handouts in order to operate profitably, it follows logically that funds must be diverted from more profitable opportunities to allow this to happen. Again, overall prosperity is reduced.

Thirdly, they can create an environment in which a free market can flourish. They can support the concept of private property so that risk takers and hard workers can retain the benefits of their labours. They can support the rule of law so that citizens can be confident that they will be treated fairly and consistently. They can support a judicial system that enforces contract law enabling citizens to trade with confidence. They can provide the transport, communications, power, water and sewerage infrastructure too.

Only in the third way do citizens as a whole benefit. The first two favour sectional interests.

Over the past two hundred years, starting in the Anglosphere but gradually spreading to other parts of the world, there have been unprecedented improvements in prosperity. One of the major contributors to this was sociological change. It became honourable to be in commerce, to work hard and to innovate. There was liberty and dignity for ordinary people. Society came to admire the entrepreneur – those who venture and invent.

In the market process, entrepreneurs are the ones who sense where opportunities are to be found. They act in the face of uncertainty to help society achieve the fullest levels of production. They assess what products or services their customers may want. They innovate to provide better products and services. They initiate productivity improvements within their own organisations. They calculate how much the proposed goods would cost to produce, how much they expect the customers to pay and how much risk is involved. If they believe that they can make a profit, commensurate with the risk, they proceed with their endeavours. To the extent that they are successful, they accumulate wealth and expertise that the business can use in future projects or to reward the shareholders for taking the risks.

Entrepreneurial talent is scarce[17]. Not everyone wants to take the risks. Not everyone has the ability or inclination. Yet their actions are essential to the prosperity of us all. People who work hard, who take risks and become well off if they succeed should be praised and encouraged.

Jobs are created by entrepreneurs. We need to honour them and to create the conditions for them to flourish.

14

THE VIRTUE OF TOLERANCE

Tolerance is an important virtue in a modern liberal democracy. This has been highlighted by the brouhaha about ultra-Orthodox Jewish men refusing to sit next to women on planes.

A story in *The New York Times* told of a woman who was asked to give up her seat on a plane because the man seated next to her held religious views that prevented his sitting next to any woman other than his wife. The woman was offended by the request and declined. There was considerable comment about this on social media, much of it short and vitriolic, but occasionally thoughtful and well-reasoned.

In essence, the conflict was between the man's right to have his religious views respected and the woman's right to be treated as an equal citizen.

In resolving this, it is important that neither party be coerced into a solution that they would not accept willingly. The airline staff should not force the man to sit next to the woman; they should not force the woman to move. Ideally, they need to find a third person willing to sit next to the woman thus freeing a suitable seat for the man. The man may need to be tolerant. He may need to accept an inferior seat in order to have his religious views accommodated.

The solution suggested most frequently on social media – that the man should avoid the problem by buying two seats – has just a hint of the intolerance that we need to avoid. My brother-in-law, an economics professor always ready with creative ideas, suggested that here was a business opportunity for the airline. They could set aside a section of the plane specifically for ultra-Orthodox Jewish men and charge a small premium for this special consideration.

Formerly, many societies shared common cultural and religious beliefs. Nowadays most societies are pluralist. The political culture of such democratic societies is marked by a diversity of opposing and irreconcilable religious, philosophical and moral disciplines. It is important to realise and accept that such views can be reasonably held[18]. Consequently, there is a need to embrace often conflicting values. You need to tolerate others' views even if you do not agree with them.

Moreover, you need to avoid inflicting your views on others. If you wish to change others' views it should be done by persuasion, never by coercion. Tolerance is needed whenever there are situations where competing values clash.

15

ELIMINATING PREJUDICE

If we work, rest and pray solely with friends who live in the same neighbourhood, we develop fears and prejudices about outsiders. But if we develop multiple associations, if we mix with people from different backgrounds, we soon realise that they too are all right. Our prejudices dissipate.

It is one hundred and fifty years since General Sherman burnt Atlanta and the American Civil War ended. Over a million lives had been lost and the Southern economy was devastated. Abe Lincoln had achieved his objectives. The USA remained one nation, and amendments to the constitution ended slavery and gave all male citizens the vote.

But laws themselves do not change attitudes. Many in the South are still smarting from the 'recent unpleasantness' and refuse to accept the changes imposed upon them. Problems of racism and social inequality persist. Cultural norms, once embedded, last for generations. Change is necessarily very slow. Multiple opportunities to mingle socially and to work together on shared tasks are required if progress is to be made.

Apartheid in South Africa and segregation in the USA failed. We should learn from these mistakes and eschew all laws based on race.

16

THE SEPARATION OF POWERS

In May 2015, in response to a suggestion that an independent body be established to evaluate infrastructure projects, the Australian Treasurer, Joe Hockey[19] said:

> The thing I'm always wary of is setting up a new independent body ... where you just give them money and they determine where the money goes, because ultimately, as a person elected by the people of Australia, I'm accountable for that.
>
> If you set up a body that has no accountability – none – no shareholders, no elections, no nothing – and they are spending billions and billions of dollars of taxpayers' money, I instinctively don't like that.

Well, I beg to disagree. I think it is essential that regulations are administered by a separate professional authority and not by members of the parliament who made the laws. Ministers should not make final decisions and administrative decisions should be subject to judicial review.

The principle of the separation of powers has been acknowledged for a long time. This is what William Paley wrote in 1785:

> The first maxim of a free state is that the laws be made by one set of men, and administered by another; in other words; that the

legislative and judicial characters be kept separate. When these offices are united in the same person or assembly, particular laws are made for particular causes, springing oftentimes from partial motives, and directed at private ends: whilst they are kept separate, general laws are made by one body of men, without foreseeing whom they may affect; and when made, must be applied by the other, let them affect whom they will.

The provision of infrastructure is an engineering discipline. The assessment of requirements involves skilled and complex mathematical modelling, taking into account what exists at the moment and the range of possible changes to usage caused by social preferences, population growth and prosperity. The delivery requires engineering skills to build for the future while maintaining current services. Planning has to be coordinated and have a generational timeframe.

Decisions on the provision of sewerage, water supply, energy, telecommunications, and road and rail networks are best made by professional bodies led by engineers and mathematicians. Having infrastructure and urban planning decisions dominated by the political process means that choices are made for short-term electoral advantage, producing sub-optimal results and piecemeal projects. A better framework is to have these services delivered by private organisations or by well-funded and empowered statutory authorities.

17

POLITICAL DONATIONS

A report in *The Age* on Tuesday 30 June 2015 claimed that the Liberal Party's fund-raising processes had been infiltrated by the Mafia to gain access to politicians and favourable decisions by ministers in relation to a visa for a gangland boss.

The immediate response has been to call for tighter controls over political donations. This would not stop the problem and would have serious consequences in a liberal democracy. Those wishing to influence political decisions will find ways around any and every regulation. Yet it would limit citizens from legitimate promotion of their political beliefs and ideologies.

To devise a satisfactory solution to any problem requires that we first gain a clear understanding of it. The problem here is not political donations per se; it is the scope of government.

Over the past century we have gradually permitted the state to assume more and more control over our lives. In particular, we have succumbed to the idea that it is legitimate for the state to take from some members of our society and give to others – to rob Peter to give to Paul. While this begins with the ideal of taking from the rich and giving to the poor, it soon degenerates into taking from those you dislike and giving to those you like, taking from those who do not vote for you and giving to those who do. It is ethically unsound. Harvard philosopher, Robert Nozick, put it well:

> Economically well-off persons desire greater political power, in a non-minimal state, because they can use this power to give themselves differential economic benefits. Where a locus of such power exists, it is not surprising that people attempt to use it for their own ends.
>
> The illegitimate use of a state by economic interests for their own ends is based upon pre-existing illegitimate power of the state to enrich some persons at the expense of others. Eliminate that illegitimate power of giving differential economic benefits and you eliminate or drastically reduce the motive for wanting political influence.[20]

Corrupt political donations will exist wherever politicians can be bought.

The solution is not to control political donations, but to control the scope of government and the limits on ministerial discretion.

18

A PETITION ON BEHALF OF THE GREEK PEOPLE[21]

I exhort the politicians and bureaucrats of Europe to think again, to do better. The Greek bailout entails too much intervention into the Greek economy and too many restrictions on the sovereignty of the Greek people. It will not work. The difficulties will endure for too long. It will all unravel.

A much better and more effective solution is possible. The Europeans should employ the well-proven and effective economic theory of *Quantitative Easing*. I am surprised Paul Krugman and Joseph Stiglitz have not already recommended this.

The European Central Bank should simply print another €400 billion. They could then use €340 billion to pay off Greece's creditors, and have a little over to provide some capital to give Greece a new start. Benefits all round. Creditors get paid. Greece becomes debt free. No austerity needed. Greeks can become proud, happy and prosperous again. Silly Maggie Thatcher proved wrong.

I am, of course, pulling your leg. You do not need a PhD in

Economics to understand that printing money cannot create wealth or repay the debts of prior profligacy.

It is worth repeating Margaret Thatcher's pithy remark, which has been much quoted in relation to the current Greek tragedy:

> The trouble with socialism is that you eventually run out of other people's money.

19

MONEY DOESN'T GROW ON TREES

My mother used to say, 'money doesn't grow on trees'. It was a common phrase for those who grew up during the Great Depression. They understood the virtue of thrift and they knew the importance of saving and investment. But now politicians and economists know better. They are much better educated and more sophisticated than my mother ever was. They are disciples of John Maynard Keynes. They read Paul Krugman in *The New York Times*.

In the USA, the world's largest economy, the government revenues from taxes are 18 per cent of GDP and their expenses are 24 per cent. The 6 per cent gap is made up by borrowing. The US Government debt is over US$19 trillion and growing – and that does not include the huge unfunded liability for social security.

Unable and unwilling to raise taxes or reduce spending, the US Congress must now increase its level of debt. Fortunately, this is quite easy. The Federal Reserve simply prints more money. So the punters don't get nervous, the politicians perplex them by calling it quantitative easing (QE). So what is all this fuss about fiscal cliffs? Surely they can continue to print money forever.

Well, there is a problem. As you print more money its unit value declines; that is, you have inflation. It may not be immediate, but it is inevitable. The burden of inflation is not born equally. It robs the savers and benefits the borrowers. It distorts investment decisions and leads to malinvestment, making everybody poorer.

The currencies of the world are all what is called 'fiat money', supported by nothing more than the reputation of the government that printed them. There was a time when they were backed by gold and before that gold was the currency of choice. The US dollar was backed by gold until 1971, when President Nixon reneged.

Since then, the world money system has been inherently unstable and could collapse at any time. I think my mother was right and Dr Bernanke was wrong.

20

LET THE MARKET SET INTEREST RATES

We rejoice when the Reserve Bank keeps interest rates on hold at their low, low levels. For we know that low interest rates encourage consumer spending and that is good for the economy. Where did we learn these fallacies? And why are they perpetuated by our politicians and financial journalists?

Australia's Prime Minister, Malcolm Turnbull, has indicated that he wants us to be optimistic about the future and his government's ability to create 'a prosperous, high-wage economy'.

A high-wage economy cannot be achieved by fiat. It cannot be achieved by increasing the minimum wage and having that flow though our industrial relations award system. The price of labour operates like all other prices. If the price is higher then there is less demand. Marginal workers are priced out of a job. This is evidenced even now where the young are denied work opportunities because the regulated price is too high. Throughout the Western world youth unemployment is typically twice the average.

Wages impact the price of all other goods and services. It will be pointless to have high wages if the price of everything we buy is also proportionally higher. To produce a prosperous high-wage economy, we need to improve the marginal productivity of the workforce. We do this by applying capital to our work.

Capital comprises the useful store of money, goods and knowledge from past work. It enables ingenuity, labour and nature to be used more effectively. It enables goods to be produced more quickly because we are not starting from scratch. We are building on the work that was done before that was not consumed. Progress requires that we spend less than we earn, and consume less than we create; that we save and invest.

We are better off than earlier generations because we are equipped with the capital goods our predecessors accumulated for us. In a modern city there is a stock of houses, factories, warehouses, offices and shops, road and rail infrastructure, supply and reticulation of gas, electricity and water, sewerage systems, telephone and internet communications and so on. Less obviously there are the systems and processes by which businesses, capital markets, courts and government operate. There is an educated and skilled workforce, experienced entrepreneurs and staff used to working in successful teams. All these contribute to making work more productive. This contributes to our prosperity.

Savings create funds for investment in new processes. Historically, it has been observed that to encourage saving we need to have interest rates at about 3 per cent above the inflation rate. Government and Central Bank control of interest rates inhibits this. The Federal Reserve in the USA has operated a zero interest rate policy since the global financial crisis. In seven years there has been no increase in productivity and wages have declined. Similar policies have led to slower growth rates in Australia in recent years.

Price controls always have deleterious effects. They reduce the quality and the quantity of the products and services affected. Price ceilings on housing rents reduce the number of properties available and ensure that maintenance is minimal. In Venezuela the price of bottled water, toilet paper and condoms are fixed by the government. Colleagues, on a recent holiday, observed that the consequence is that these products are generally available only on the black market.

Controls on interest rates are the worst. Interest rates are the most important price in a market economy. They have an impact on everything else. If interest rates are set artificially low, then there will be insufficient saving. Then there will be insufficient investment. Consequently, there will be a decline in the capital available to increase the marginal productivity of our workforce.

If we want to be prosperous, we need to let interest rates be set by the market, not the Reserve Bank.

21

CITIZENSHIP

New laws are proposed to strip citizenship from those who oppose our principles and our way of life – specifically those who go overseas and fight for ISIS.

This gives us pause for thought. What do we believe in? What are the characteristics that define what it is to be Australian? To what extent might one hold different views but still remain a citizen? If we define clearly what is required of an Australian citizen, might this impact our immigration policy?

New citizens are asked to commit to the following:

> I pledge my loyalty to Australia and its people, whose democratic beliefs I share, whose rights and liberties I respect, and whose laws I will uphold and obey.

Is this tightly written oath sufficient? Would it unravel if one attempted to expand it?

Australia's cultural values and laws are based on the heritage of Western civilization. At the heart of this is a belief in democracy – that all people have equal political rights – and the rule of law – that everyone, including the state, is accountable to laws that are publicly promulgated, equally enforced and independently adjudicated.

These values distinguish us from many other nations of the world. They contribute significantly to our freedom and our prosperity. Public discussion of what it means to be Australian will be valuable. It will help us appreciate how lucky we are. It will inform our security and immigration policies.

We should not take citizenship for granted.

22

A CALIPHATE IS NOT THE ANSWER

At the Hizb ut-Tahrir conference in Sydney on 1 November 2015 speakers complained of the oppressive campaign of forced assimilation being waged against them by the Australian government, evidenced by the requirement to sing the national anthem and pledge support for democratic values in the citizenship oath.

Hizb ut-Tahrir is an Islamic political party whose professed aim is to create a caliphate where all Muslims can live under sharia law. They believe that society should be governed by the rule of god not the rule of man, and are therefore opposed to democracy.

I have no issue with their holding this belief provided that they do not use force to impose it on others. I believe that citizens should achieve their desires through rational persuasion and never through violence, coercion or political influence.

Our liberties are based on certain rights that have been developed and refined over many centuries. These include our rights to free speech; to our religious and political beliefs; to choose our friends and associates, and whom we may marry; to choose our occupation; to choose where we may live; to choose what we may eat or drink or wear; to choose our entertainments; to own private property, that is, to retain the rewards from our work and to dispose of them as we see fit; to form voluntary associations; to equal protection under the law; to habeas corpus, that is not to be detained unlawfully; to be able to enter into legally enforceable contracts; and so on.

Elsewhere in the world, where these values are not the norm, people are oppressed and live in poverty. Their societies lack compassion and civility. There is no creative drive to improve their spiritual, cultural and economic well-being. There are no opportunities for young people to learn, to grow and to develop their talents to the full.

Ours is a secular, pluralistic society that embraces people of diverse cultures and religious backgrounds. To be a citizen in our society requires adherence to our core values. For this to work requires tolerance. Many differences can be accommodated within our democratic framework. But we cannot accept that some citizens are outside the law; that they have laws of their own.

If our friends in Hizb ut-Tahrir wish to live under a caliphate, and to live under sharia law, then they will have to do it elsewhere. Such a society cannot be accommodated in democratic Australia.

23

THE FIGHT AGAINST JIHADIST ISLAMISM

If we wish to convince others that our ideology is superior, then firstly we must understand its concepts and its roots, and secondly we must live its truth.[22]

We live in one of the freest and most prosperous societies in the history of mankind. This has not happened by chance. It is due to the institutions we inherited from Britain: the rule of law; the principle of private property, a free enterprise economy, a culture that accepts a wide range of human rights – to free speech, to political and religious beliefs, to choose whom we may marry, and so on. Our freedoms and prosperity are also enhanced by living in a democratic society where all men and women are equal before the law and have an equal opportunity to contribute.

These are what distinguish us from the totalitarian regimes which deliver poverty, destroy trust among their citizens, and terrorize, censor and imprison or kill those who disagree with the party line.

Today, jihadist Islamism[23] presents us with a clash of ideologies. While we may attempt to combat this militarily and politically, the real battle will be in the realm of ideas.

Tomorrow on your train to work there may be a stranger with a suicide vest. Or when you meet a friend for coffee, a stranger may enter the café with an AK47 and shoot you and your friend and all the other pagans. Paris on Friday 13 November stays with you forever. You live in fear.

Your government promises to protect you. They bomb Raqqa. They close the borders to refugees. They equip police to intercept everyone's phone calls and search their homes without a warrant. Security checks at airports become more thorough and take twice as long.

But the stranger does not come from Raqqa. He is not a refugee. He is unknown to police. He is just a guy who believes passionately in jihadist Islamism. He yearns for a theocratic caliphate. He believes that all states should conform to sharia law and that all people should convert to his version of Islam. He believes in the use of force to spread his views.

While the stranger is Muslim, that alone does not define him. Most Muslims are peaceful citizens who can and do participate productively in society. The stranger is hard to identify; his distinguishing features are inside his head.

Our wonderful, free and prosperous society is being threatened by ideologies, from within and without, that compromise the reasons for its success. If we are to succeed in our battle with competing ideologies, then we need to acquire an appreciation of the legacy of our Western civilization and be determined to live up to its ideals.

BIBLIOGRAPHY

Bastiat, C.F. (2011). *The Bastiat Collection*. Auburn: Ludwig von Mises Institute.

Harris, S. & Nawaz, M. (2015). *Islam and the Future of Tolerance*. Cambridge, Massachusetts: Harvard University Press.

Havel, V. (1992). *Summer Meditations*. London: Faber and Faber.

Hayek, F.A. (2007). *The Road to Serfdom*. London: University of Chicago Press.

Hazlitt, H. (1979). *Economics in One Lesson*. New York: Three Rivers Press.

John Paul II. (1991). *Centesimus Annus*. Rome: Libreria Editrice Vaticana.

Mises, L. v. (2008). *Human Action*. Auburn: Ludwig von Mises Institute.

Nozick, R. (1974). *Anarchy, State, and Utopia*. Oxford: Basil Blackwell.

Paul, R. (2009). *End the Fed*. New York: Grand Central Publishing.

Rawls, J. (1996). *Political Liberalism*. New York: Columbia University Press.

Rothbard, M.N. (2002). *The Ethics of Liberty*. New York: New York University Press.

Rothbard, M.N. (2005). *What Has Government Done to Our Money?* Auburn: Ludwig von Mises Institute.

Woods, T.E. (2010). *Back on the Road to Serfdom*. Wilmington: ISI Books.

MISES INSTITUTE

The Mises Institute is a boutique private university, specializing in libertarian philosophy and Austrian economics. It is named after Ludwig von Mises, one of the towering intellects of the twentieth century. It is located in Auburn, Alabama – a small university town with a large football stadium. The population is only 80,000, of whom 30,000 are at the university

The Mises Institute offers fellowships, research grants, opportunities to publish in scholarly journals, academic conferences and access to its extensive libraries to scholars from all around the world. Through its summer schools and graduate seminars, it has helped thousands of students. For the general public, it offers numerous publications, seminars, online classes, videos and a daily blog – all free of charge.

There are lecture rooms and extensive libraries – over 40,000 volumes, including Murray Rothbard's personal library. There are private study rooms for academics and PhD students. A most significant feature of the campus is the numerous discussion areas – many of them in the open – where students can debate among themselves and with their professors. In a very personal and intimate touch, there are busts of its heroes – Mises, of course, but also F.A. Hayek, Murray Rothbard, Henry Hazlitt and Leonard E. Read.

If you would like to know more about libertarian philosophy and Austrian economics, the Mises Institute is your ideal source. You can find them at www.mises.org.

ABOUT PETER FRANCIS FENWICK

I was born in Geelong, Australia and educated at The Geelong College. I studied Civil Engineering at the Gordon Institute of Technology in Geelong, and Melbourne University, graduating in 1966. In 1972 I completed an MBA with distinction at Melbourne University.

From 1976 to 2011 I ran a successful consulting business, Fenwick Software, which implements commercial systems for business in the manufacturing, distribution, and waste management recycling industries. I have established an employee shareholder scheme and five of my long-term staff now own 75 per cent, and manage the business. I remain chairman of the company.

At Melbourne University, I studied philosophy under the charismatic Father Eric Darcy. I am an alumnus of the Cranlana colloquium, a facilitated program, inspired by the Aspen Institute in the USA, designed to promote open and informed, non-partisan dialogue on the philosophical, ethical and social issues central to creating a just, prosperous and sustainable society. My philosophies were given practical expression in the culture and practices of my consulting business.

I have been married to Jill, a schoolteacher and author, since 1966. We have three sons and three grandchildren. We live in East Melbourne, Australia.

BOOKS BY PETER FRANCIS
FENWICK

My first book was The Fragility of Freedom: Why Subsidiarity Matters. It was published in 2014 by Connor Court.

Referencing the work of over fifty great political philosophers and economists, The Fragility of Freedom explores the theory that underpins our systems of liberty, prosperity and justice. It examines how progress has been constrained by the errors of the dominant political ideologies of the twentieth century and how opportunities have been squandered.

It proposes a moral society, based on the principle of subsidiarity, in which individuals take responsibility for themselves and their families, where voluntary organisations thrive, and the state plays a limited role.

You can find it in paperback and eBook editions at your favourite bookstore.

ENDNOTES

1 Libertarianism was formerly called Liberalism. Unfortunately, the term was usurped by the Social Democrats and now the term 'liberal' has the opposite meaning to its original one – particularly in the USA. Sometimes the term 'classical liberalism' is used, but it has now become common to use libertarianism to describe this philosophy.

2 Mary Wollstonecraft, a contemporary of Thomas Paine, was a libertarian writer two hundred years ahead of her time. In *A Vindication of the Rights of Women (1792)* – a response to Rousseau's *Emile* which proposed that a woman's education should aim at making her useful to and supportive of a rational man – she proposed that women should seek *reason* over *sensibility*. In her later writing, she grappled with the need of women for companionship and freedom to express their sexuality, as well as for reason and independence.

3 The famous Hans Christian Andersen fable tells of the weavers who create a suit for their vain emperor which they say is invisible to those who are incompetent or stupid. No-one dares to admit that they see no clothes, so all remain silent. An innocent child is the only one prepared to state the obvious – that the emperor is naked.

4 Tom Woods is a senior fellow at the Mises Institute in Auburn, Alabama and the author of nine books including *The Politically Incorrect Guide to American History*, *The Church and the Market: A Catholic Defense of the Free Economy* and *Meltdown* – his analysis of the 2008 crash. The quotation is from his introduction to *Back on the Road to Serfdom*, which he edited.

5 F.A. Hayek, *The Road to Serfdom*, p.65

6 Y. Levin, Beyond *the Welfare State*, Issue No. 7, Spring 2011, National Affairs. Yuval Levin is a political analyst and journalist. He is the author of *Tyranny of Reason*, *Imagining the Future* and *The Great Debate: Edmund Burke, Thomas Paine, and the Birth of Right and Left*. He has a PhD from the University of Chicago.

7 Peter Francis Fenwick, *The Fragility of Freedom*, p 2

8 Paul Krugman is a Nobel Prize winning economist who writes a column *The Conscience of a Liberal* for *The New York Times*. He promotes a Keynesian view.

9 Per Bylund, *How the Welfare State Corrupted Sweden*, Mises Daily, May 31, 2006.

10 Geoff Bartlett is Australia's pre-eminent sculptor. He is represented in the National Gallery of Australia, the National Gallery of Victoria, the Art Gallery of New South Wales, Parliament House Art Collection, and Heide Museum of Modern Art, and in many regional, university, corporate and private collections. He has a Master of Fine Arts (Hons) from Columbia University, New York.

11 Robert Nozick, *Anarchy, State & Utopia*, p 272

12 Australian Council of Trade Unions

13 From 1934 to 1946, Henry Hazlitt was the principal editorial writer on finance and economics for the *New York Times*. He then wrote a column in *Newsweek* for twenty years. He was instrumental in introducing Mises and Hayek to an American audience. He was the founding Vice-President of the Foundation for Economic Education and an original member of the Mount Pelerin Society. He wrote 25 books. *Economics in One Lesson*, from which the following quotation is taken, is his enduring legacy. In it he explains the basic truths of economics in language that a layman can understand.

14 Karol Josef Wojtyla made history in 1978 when he became John-Paul II - the first non-Italian pope in 400 years. He was a vocal advocate for human rights. He travelled the world, visiting more than 100 countries to spread his message of faith and peace, and to use his influence to bring about political change. He played a role in the fall of communism in his native Poland. He was an intellectual pope, with a profound understanding of economics. In his 1991 encyclical, *Centesimus Annus*, Pope John-Paul praises democracy and a free market economy, and explicitly rejects socialism. At the same time, he highlights the dangers when man's spiritual dimensions are subordinated to his material ones.

15 Peter Drucker was a prolific writer, consultant and teacher. He had a profound

influence on the theory of management and the role of the manager in society. He invented management by objectives and he coined the term 'knowledge worker'. He explained that the goal to maximise profit was a false one for the businessman – it provided no guide for action - whereas to create a customer guided everything. He wrote about forty books, most of which are still in print. My favourites are:The Practice of Management (1954), Managing for Results (1964), The Effective Executive (1967).

16 Vaclav Havel, *Summer Meditations*, p. 67.

17 Steve Jobs is undoubtedly the most famous entrepreneur of the twentieth century. His innovative Apple products have transformed our lives. He had an amazing feel for what the customer wanted. He once told engineers designing the Macintosh to get rid of the noise. They explained that it was the fan, and the fan was required to cool the disc. He told them to fix it and stormed out. Thirty years later, I purchased a MacBook Air for my wife. It has no disc, just solid state memory. It is quiet. Just like she expects it to be. Drucker would have applauded.

18 John Rawls addresses this problem in *Political Liberalism*.

19 Joe Hockey is now the Australian Ambassador to the USA.

20 Robert Nozick is regarded as one of the two most influential political philosophers of the twentieth century. The other was his Harvard colleague John Rawls. The above quotation is taken from his most famous work, *Anarchy, State, and Utopia*. In it, Nozick reflects a libertarian position to which he adds the moral one: the respect for individual rights that flow from man's inherent human dignity, his self-ownership.

21 The title pays homage to Frederic Bastiat, the great nineteenth century French economist and his famous *Petition on behalf of the Manufacturers of Candles, Waxlights. Lamps, Candlelights, Street Lamps, Snuffers, Extinguishers, and the Producers of Oil, Tallow, Resin, Alcohol, and, generally, of Everything Connected with Lighting*. Bastiat's essay was a witty demolition of arguments in favour of protective tariffs. It is still relevant today. His work is still in print.

22 This is an edited version of a letter to the editor published in the January-February 2016 edition of *Quadrant*.

23 The dialogue between Sam Harris and Maajid Nawaz, *Islam and the Future of Tolerance*, is a most informative book for anyone who wishes to understand the current crises caused by jihadist Islamism. Nawaz makes the important distinction between the religion that is Islam and the political ideology that is Islamism. He defines Islamism as a desire to impose any given interpretation of Islam on society, and jihadism as the intent to spread it by force. Sam Harris asks the tough questions. Maajid Nawaz, because of his experiences and his intelligence, provides informed answers.

www.ingramcontent.com/pod-product-compliance
Lightning Source LLC
Chambersburg PA
CBHW072210270326

41930CB00011B/2603